MW01612310

Statement to the Trustees of the Worcester Polytechnic Institute

From C. G. Washburn

STATEMENT

TO THE TRUSTEES OF THE

WORCESTER POLYTECHNIC INSTITUTE

By C. G. WASHBURN

OCTOBER 16, 1908

STATEMENT

TO THE TRUSTEES OF THE

WORCESTER POLYTECHNIC INSTITUTE

By C G WASHBURN

OCTOBER 15, 1908

WORCESTER, MASS
THE COMMONWEALTH PRESS
50 FOSTER STREET
1908

October 12, 1908.

To the Trustees of the Worcester Polytechnic Institute:

The Treasurer's report for the year ending April 30, 1908, has been placed in your hands, from which it appears that the combined income of the School and Shop was $164,275 and the combined expenditure $180,726, showing a deficit of $16,451. These figures do not include anything but cash receipts and disbursements and it is obvious that the fact that part of the deficit is attributable to investment in equipment does not make less serious the condition, because it is essential that our cash receipts should at least equal our cash disbursements. Of this deficit of $16,451, $10,210 has been invested in equipment. Since the establishment of the school and exclusive of the equipment of The Washburn Shops, equipment has been supplied out of the current income of the school which had an inventory value January 1, 1908, of $224,216.83. During the fifteen fiscal years ending April 30, 1908, there has been a surplus in the years 1894, 1896 and 1897. In all the other years there has been a deficit and the average amount of the deficit has been about $14,000.

The financial condition of the Institute has been a cause of anxiety for some years. For example: in my report as Treasurer of April 30, 1904, I called attention to the fact that for five years ending April 30, 1904, the average annual deficit had been $15,997, and that for some time the Trustees had been considering in what way our revenues could be increased. Something has been accomplished in this direction by the increase by the Legislature of 1905 in the annual payment to cover forty free State scholarships from $6,000 to $10,000.

Dr. Engler, on April 29, 1905, made a very full report to the Trustees, which was printed under date of May 6th, 1905, in which he took the position that if we had $300,000 to expend it would be much wiser to expend it in enlarging our facilities

4

than in investing it in securities and increasing our income by say, $12,000 a year, the general theory being that the cost per student decreases as the number of students increases up to a certain number which gives the maximum of economy, and that with an attendance of 650, the Institute would be self-sustaining upon the then present endowment, and that with an attendance of 825 the tuitions alone would support the Institute. He estimated that the attendance would probably be 390 in 1905-6 and 450 in 1906-7. We did not have the funds at that time to warrant us in acting upon Dr. Engler's recommendations.

At the June 3, 1905, meeting Mr. Salisbury announced his intention to resign as President, and also his desire to place $100,000 at the disposal of the Trustees. This $100,000 we said at the time would enable us to return the $81,000 we had borrowed from principal, and the $20,000 we had expended for equipment, and to start square with the world.

Mr. Salisbury died Nov. 16, 1905, and his will contained a bequest of $200,000. This, in addition to the gift of $100,000, placed $300,000 at our disposal, and under date of November 29, 1905, the Trustees, through the Executive Committee, authorized the expenditure for a new building and equipment in addition to that already made. We also put motors in The Washburn Shops and the Mechanical Laboratory at an expenditure of $3,000, and June 9, 1906, made a special appropriation of $2,500 for new apparatus on the first floor of the Laboratory.

In my Treasurer's report of April 29, 1905, I called attention to the fact that we had raised to pay running expenses in addition to our current income the sum of $81,552 from the following sources:

Securities sold,	$28,802
Notes outstanding,	49,000
Loan from principal,	3,750
	$81,552

To this should be added deficit for year ending

April 30, 1906,	$4,032
April 30, 1907,	17,037
April 30, 1908,	16,451
Total deficit to " " "	$119,072

To meet this deficit and to cover the cost of erecting and equipping the new Electrical Engineering Laboratory with attendant changes in the Chemical Laboratory and the Power House which cost $218,473, more or less, we have had Mr. Salisbury's gift of $100,000 and the legacy of $200,000,— $300,000 in all to cover a deficit and expenditures of $337,545, so that including other items our resources are impaired by our various operations, as of April 30, 1908, to the amount of $53,642. See page 17, Treasurer's 1908 report.

Referring now to the matter of attendance, I would remind the Trustees that Dr. Engler, in his printed report, made certain estimates which have been extended to 1910-11. I give below the estimated attendance and the actual attendance, together with the quotation from Dr. Engler's letter to me of August 24th, 1908, in regard to the matter.

"From this it appears that the attendance will be approximately as shown in the first column following. The actual attendance to date is given in the second column.

	Estimated	Actual
1905-'06	390	388
1906-'07	450	437
1907-'08	——	465
1908-'09	520	487
1909-'10	600	——
1910-'11	650	——

"For the year 1905-'06, the approach of the actual to the estimated attendance is so close that no explanation is needed. For the year 1906-'07, I think that there is no doubt that the failure to reach the estimate is largely due to our tardiness in providing increased facilities. For the year 1907-8, the attendance would undoubtedly have reached 500 or thereabouts (although no prediction was made in my statement of April 29th, 1905), had we not increased our entrance requirements by requiring an amount of preparation which represents two additional years in the preparatory school, and this went into effect for the first time for the year 1906-'07. This, you will recall, was done under pressure, in order to meet the requirements for the Carnegie Foundation for the Advancement for Teaching, and done deliberately, although it was well recognized that it would tend to check for a time the rate of increase.

"If further additional facilities, such as gymnasium, auditorium, etc., can be supplied in the near future, I think there is no doubt that we shall reach an attendance of 650, by the year 1910-'11, as shown above.

"It is, of course, to be understood, that these curves are drawn on the supposition that facilities will be provided as they are needed. If this is not done, so rapid a growth as shown cannot be expected."

The cost of instruction, including the cost of the office, has increased from $50,700, in 1903-4, to $69,194, in 1907-8. The following table will show the figures in detail. The salaries of the four Shop instructors are not included in this table. During this time the number of students has increased from 272 to 465, and the amount of tuitions received, excluding the grant from the State, from $26,470 to $61,043.

COST OF INSTRUCTION, WORCESTER POLYTECHNIC INSTITUTE.

Department,	1903-04.	1904-05.	1905-06.	1906-07.	1907-08.
Office,	$7,100	$7,100	$7,100	$8,144	$8,144
Mathematics,	5,000	5,000	5,750	5,750	6,375
Chemistry,	7,700	8,700	8,700	8,900	9,300
Economics and Political Science,	2,000	2,000	2,000	2,000	2,500
Language,	3,500	3,500	3,500	3,500	4,375
Electrical Engineering,	5,200	6,700	8,900	8,910	11,300
Civil Engineering,	3,300	4,300	4,300	5,100	5,800
Physics,	3,700	4,400	4,400	5,500	5,500
Mechanical, Engineering,	12,600	12,800	13,000	15,400	15,400
Library,	600	600	600	600	600
Total,	$50,700	$55,100	$58,250	$63,804	$69,194

In reviewing the financial history of the Institute, two facts are very striking : the first, that the endowment should have increased so little ; and the second, that so few individuals should have contributed to the resources of the school. It would seem as if an institution of this sort would be sympathetically regarded by a large number of people in a manufacturing community like this. The lack of a large number of contributors, I think may, in part, be explained by the fact that the Institute has been regarded as one of Mr. Salisbury's peculiar charges, and the feeling has been widely held that he would provide all the funds necessary for the development of the school. That he and his father did much for the Institute, is a fact that we all recognize, and we should also recognize the fact, and the community must be brought to realize, that nothing further from that source can be received, and an effort should be made to bring the needs of the Institute to the attention of the public spirited business men of Worcester.

Our income from invested funds in 1873, was $27,540, the largest amount received from this source in any year. In 1901 the income from invested funds, was $27,466. So that it is quite within the truth to say, that for a period of thirty years the income from invested funds has remained stationary. I do not make the comparison with the four earlier years of the history of the Institute, because of the fact that the endowment funds were not then thoroughly established.

In marked contrast with the income from invested funds, is the income from tuitions, which, beginning with $120 in 1869, only amounted to $5,269, in 1890. From 1872 to 1876, inclusive, tuitions averaged about $1,500 a year, while in the eighteen years since 1890, income from tuitions has increased from $5,269 to $61,043, it is therefore apparent that the increasing needs of the school have been met exclusively out of tuitions, supplemented by state aid, which, as appears in another part of this communication, now amounts to $10,000 annually. It should be added here by way of explanation that September 16, 1868, the tuition was fixed at $60.00 per year, and no resident of Worcester County paid any tuition. In 1871, the tuition was increased to $100 per year, 1880 to $150, where it now remains, with a laboratory fee of $10.00 in addition.

By vote of April 20, 1889, free tuition to students of Worcester County was limited to the income from the Boynton fund of $100,000.

The estimated attendance of 520 in 1908-09, has not been realized, the actual attendance as of September 24, 1908, being 482. This falling off is attributed by Dr. Engler, to hard times. Based on this attendance, the probable deficit in the Academic department for the year ending April 30, 1909, will be about $13,500. In this estimate The Washburn Shops account has not been considered, and, of course, it is impossible now to say, whether, or not, our collections will equal our expenditures, but for the four months, May to August, inclusive, in the present fiscal year, the Shop expenditures have exceeded the Shop collections, by the amount of $5,241. It is true that this has been a time of great business depression, and these are the less active business months of the year; but, assuming that the deficit in the Shop should be no greater, it would make our total deficit in both departments, for the year ending April 30, 1909, in the vicinity of $18,500.

If our estimated attendance of 650 should be reached in 1910-11, which we have regarded as the self-sustaining number of students, we should reach that point in the following financial condition.

Impairment of Resources to April 30, 1908,	$53,642
Estimated deficit, 1908-9,	18,500
Estimated deficit, 1909-10,	18,500
	$90,642

That is to say, we shall reach the self-sustaining period with a deficit amounting, in round numbers, to $90,000, and in the event that we should be disappointed in our expectations, and the self-sustaining period should not be reached so soon, our financial condition would, of course, be still less favorable. It should also be borne in mind that we must expect some increase in salaries from year to year, some extraordinary expenditures which cannot be foreseen, and it would occur to any prudent person that the forecast I am making is probably more favorable than the facts, when they are ascertained, will warrant.

All this points to the immediate necessity of increasing our endowment by not less than $500,000. Just how this can be accomplished I am not prepared to say, and it is a matter that will require careful consideration.

The fact is that the Institute has developed far beyond the plan of its founders, and has ceased to be, almost exclusively, a local institution. Whereas in 1870-1 a little over 6% of the students were from outside of the Commonwealth of Massachusetts, in 1907-8 the percentage has increased to nearly 30%. These figures would appear to warrant us in going outside of the Commonwealth in an attempt to increase our endowment. In this connection I desire again to call the attention of the Trustees to a copy of letter from Dr. Engler, dated October 1, 1907, in regard to the future of the Institute. This letter was laid before the Trustees at the October, 1907, meeting, but no action has ever been taken thereon, and I print it herewith. I also append hereto a statement of the value of the property of the Institute of April 30, 1908, and from what sources it has been received, also a statement showing the income and expenditures of the school each year since its foundation and a similar statement for the Shop, and a statement showing what we have contributed to the Commonweath of Massachusetts in the excess over our receipts in grants of the actual cost of educating the students.

CHARLES G. WASHBURN,
President.

WORCESTER POLYTECHNIC INSTITUTE
OFFICE OF THE PRESIDENT
WORCESTER, MASS.,
Oct. 1, 1907.

MR. CHARLES G. WASHBURN,
> President, Board of Trustees,
>> Worcester Polytechnic Institute,
>>> Worcester, Mass.

DEAR MR. WASHBURN, (Copy)

As you are doubtless aware, the courses of study at the Worcester Polytechnic Institute, in common with the courses of study at other similar institutions, have from the beginning been going through a process of evolution, which process has perhaps been more rapid and more significant during recent years than earlier.

The general trend of this evolution has been one of continuous advance from the grade of a school slightly, if at all in advance of the existing High School, to the present grade of an engineering school of the first rank.

We have recently, as you know, raised our entrance requirements until now they are as high and as severe as those of any engineering school in the country. The courses of study in the Institute have been enlarged and enriched during the course of years, until now our graduates stand on a par with the graduates of the best technical schools in the United States.

It seems to me that the time has come to consider the future, and that it is very desirable that we should take a long look ahead, in order to direct the course of the subsequent evolution in those channels which will prove to be the best for the development of the institution as well as for the future of technical education in the United States.

Until now we have attempted, as every other engineering school in the country has attempted, to give in four years' time the essentials (whatever that may mean) of a so-called liberal education and at the same time the foundations, at least, of technical training in the particular line in which the student desires to specialize. We are well aware that this attempt has been at best only partially successful in the case of most individual students, and wholly successful in only very few cases. Yet the necessities of the situation have compelled all technical schools to adopt some general method. It has been heretofore, and is now, found impossible to give the necessary preparation for a strictly technical training in any of the preparatory schools which have existed in the country, thus placing upon the technical schools the burden of supplying such deficiencies in general education as appear in the student's training when he comes from the preparatory school, and at the same time enable him to enter upon his profession with a sound and sufficiently broad technical training to enable him to meet commercial competition.

In the meantime the demands upon the technically trained man have been growing at a rapid rate on account of the great and various advances which have been made in the application of scientific knowledge to the everyday demands of civilized life. Specialization in the various lines has become a necessity, and special knowledge and training are demanded in many fields where formerly no training was obtainable or necessary. The general tendency has been, and is now, more evidently than ever before, to demand that the engineer in any line shall be a strictly professional and professionally trained man, in the same sense that the lawyer or the physician is a professionally trained man. The response of the technical schools to this demand has until now consisted in the enlargement and enrichment of the courses of study, but there is already clear indication that in the very near future the engineering courses must be made strictly professional if the demands of the times are to be met by the schools. The school which first announces that its engineering courses are to be strictly professional, and provides the necessary instruction and facilities to make them so, will thereby at once secure a prestige which could not be secured in any other way, and would be recognized as a leader in technical education. Such projects are already under consideration in some of the great Universities which have technical departments, and some others which have no technical departments are contemplating the inauguration of strictly professional engineering departments.

It will be necessary for the Worcester Polytechnic Institute to decide in the not very distant future whether its development shall proceed in the direction above indicated, or whether we shall remain as we now are and leave the advance which I have indicated for other institutions to take.

The Institute is in a position to place itself upon a strictly professional basis for its courses without any serious change in its present methods, or any great derangement of its courses. As you know, until recently the students were required to decide which course they would choose when they entered the Freshman Class; but in recent years the Freshman course has been made common to all students and they are not required to choose their course of study until the end of the Freshman Year. It would be easily possible to arrange a suitable course of study, which should be common to all students during the first two years, and which would include all subjects of a general and fundamental character, such as General Chemistry, Physics, Mathematics, Languages, and the like, and which would give adequate preparation for any of the technical courses to be pursued later. This plan is already in operation in some of the engineering schools. If this were done the third and fourth years could be devoted more strictly than they are now to professional work, and would enable us to register more conveniently and with less irregularity than at present

12

advanced students from other engineering schools and from colleges giving general courses, like Amherst, Williams, Bates, Bowdoin, etc., and from industrial schools which are developing in Massachusetts and elsewhere.

Looking still further ahead, it may become desirable in the future, at such time as increased general registration and increased registration of graduate students under the operation of the step already outlined and the necessary financial support will justify such action, to abolish the granting of the Bachelor of Science Degree at the end of four years and to grant the Engineering Degrees at the end of a three years' professional course, for which professional course we would prepare our own men by the two preparatory years, and to which graduates of general colleges and others of corresponding attainment could be admitted without difficulties.

It seems to be only a question of time when the Institute will be compelled to place itself upon the general basis outlined above or consent to take second place in the rank of engineering schools.

My object to calling attention to this matter now is not that any decisive action should be taken at present, but to ascertain, if possible, whether it is considered good policy for the Institute to proceed in the development which has already begun, or whether it is to be checked in its natural development and leave the higher field to other schools.

I consider it highly important that any changes in the courses of study which may be made in the near future, for some of which no doubt suggestions will come from faculty action very soon, should be made in accordance with a well-defined general plan rather than for expediency to meet emergencies. In any case the changes which would be necessary to accomplish the result outlined above, must be gradual, and I think the transition from our present status to that of a strictly professional school could be made in the course of a few years without causing any special commotion. We are in as good a position to make this change as any institution in the country with which I am acquainted.

Yours very truly,

(Signed) EDMUND A. ENGLER,

President.

Value of property, real and personal,	$1,325,867.85
of which the Commonwealth has contributed	200,000.00
and individuals resident in the	
County and City of Worcester	1,125,867.85
Net amount of income producing funds	596,456.85
Invested in real estate and equipment	729,411.00

APPROPRIATIONS

Heretofore Made by Commonwealth.

1869. $ 50,000 upon condition that twenty free scholarships should be maintained. This sum was expended upon the plant.

1886. $ 50,000 without condition, which has been made a part of the endowment known as the "State Fund."

1894. $100,000 paid one-half in 1894, the other half in 1895; expended on buildings and equipment.

1896. An annual payment of $3,000 from September 1, 1896, conditioned upon forty free scholarships, including those provided for in the appropriation of 1869.

1899. An annual payment of $6,000 (in place of $3,000) from September 1, 1899, to cover the forty free scholarships provided for in the Act of 1896.

1905. An annual payment of $10,000 (in place of $6,000) from September 1, 1905, to cover forty free scholarships.

The only aid now being received by the Institute from the Commonwealth is the annual payment of $10,000 to cover the forty free scholarships which are maintained at an annual expense approximating $12,000.

ACADEMIC DEPARTMENT.

Year ending June I	From tuitions	From Invested funds	Amounting to	Total income	Expenditures	Equipment	Surplus	Deficit
1869	$ 120	$ 7,645	$ 7,765	$ 9,264	$14,504			$ 5240
1870	411	14,376	14,787	65,287a	19,439		$45,848a	
1871	794	19,173	19,967	20,484	17,739		2,745	
1872	1,776	20,293	22,069	22,331	21,066		1,265	
1873	1,250	27,540	28,790	30,099	25,321		4,778	
1874	1,625	25,043	26,668	26,747	26,117		630	
1875	1,300	24,840	26,140	26,149	28,024			1,875
1876	1,950	23,885	25,835	25,934	30,768			4,834
1877	1,800	22,055	23,855	27,355b	31,302			3,947
1878	1,400	21,301	22,701	24,701b	26 432			1,731
1879	1,400	19,795	21,195	21,195c	31,841			10,646
April 30,								
1880	700	19,494	20,194	24,194	22,794	1,400		
1881	2,720	18,890	21,610	22,768	22,788			20
1882	3,675	19,989	23,664	34,664d	25,967	8,697		
1883	3,000	18,580	21,580	21,580	22,584			1,004
1884	6,535	19,576	26,111	29,627e	28,148	1,479		
1885	5,638	21,604	27,242	28,011	29,774			1,763
1886	6,005	23,194	29,199	29,829	30,487			658
1887	5,298	24,298	29,596	30,446	30,658			212
1888	6,193	26,131	32,324	32,965	31,601	1,364		
1889	5,487	25,381	30,868	31,238	31,169	69		
1890	5,269	24,963	30,232	30,938	35,128			4,190
1891	12,357	24,364	36,721	37,441	37,040	401		
1892	16,129	24,847	40,966	42,424	41,658	766		
1893	23,935	25,103	49,038	50,319	48,114	2,205		
1894	28,464	25,329	53,793	56,150	52,219	3,931		
1895	24,201	24,637	48,838	49,454	54,960			5,506
1896	23,504	24,512	48,016	48,958	56,560			7,602
1897	23,767	25,625	49,392	54,795	59,916			5,121
1898	22,742	24,624	47,366	51,776	63,615			11,839
1899	25,632	27,158	52,790	57,629	60,214	$ 1,688		2,585
1900	28,050	25,876	53,926	61,853	58,262	7,201	3,591	
1901	28,360	27,466	55,826	63,386	61,988	4,672	1,398	
1902	28,787	26,766	55,553	63,235	67,936	7,750		4,701
1903	24,500	24,621	49,121	58,451	73,892	5,467		15,441
1904	26,470	24,203	50,673	62,029	73,264	5,720		11,235
1905	36,739	24,139	60,878	71,413	77,087	6,177		5,674
1906	43,770	25,573	69,343	82,563	90,345	4,482		7,782
1907	53,372	24,807	78,179	89,594	114,275	15,555		24,681
1908	61,043	25,017	86,060	99,817	120,331	10,219		20,514
	$596,168	$922,703	$1,518,871	$1,717,093	$1,795,327	$68,931	$80,567	$158,801

a. State Appropriation, $50,000.   b.   Gift of Mr. Knowlton, $2,000.   c.   Gifts, $4,000.
d.   Gifts, $11,000.   e.   Gifts from trustees and others, $3,507.

THE WASHBURN SHOPS.

	Tuitions	Income	Collections	Total Receipts	Expenditures	Cash Balance	Surplus	Deficit
1870				$ 14,032	$ 13,826	$ 206	$ 206	
1871		$ 4,070	$ 4,964	17,354	13,991	3,563	3,363	
1872		5,718	14,224	19,942	22,273	1,232		2,331
1873	$ 450	2,408	11,438	19,788x	20,022	998		234
1874	400	3,500	10,274	15,785y	16,782			997
1875	200	3,500	16,751	20,451	20,082z	369	369	
1876	50	3,450	12,179	15,675	17,046	-1,002n		1,371
1877	350	3,300	16,909	20,559	19,389	168	1,170	
1878	250	3,300	19,297	22,847	19,089	3,926	3,758	
1879	200	3,300	14,010	17,510	15,751	5,684	1,759	
1880	375	3,300	4,749	8,424	7,741	5,620	683	
1881		3,066	21,321	24,387	22,244	6,823	2,143	
1882		2,283	23,832	26,116	27,430	5,508		1,314
1883		2,550	33,164	35,714	37,843	3,379		2,129
1884	825	2,601	17,806	22,137	23,293	2,258		1,156
1885	1,200	2,458	16,540	20,383	20,998	1,643		615
1886	825	2,551	18,418	21,793	22,652	784		859
1887	675	2,588	21,864	25,127	24,509	1,402	618	
1888	750	2,927	29,568	38,246b	35,096	4,552	3,150	
1889	375	3,016	29,565	32,956	31,919	5,590	1,037	
1890	2,550	3,067	31,220	36,838	40,909	1,519		4,071
1891	1,575	2,907	47,362	54,844c	52,553	3,810	2,291	
1892	4,070	2,850	68,987	79,907d	79,843	3,874	64	
1893	4,575	2,625	81,327	88,528	81,303	11,099	7,225	
1894	3,000	2,896	78,612	84,508	74,722	20,885	9,786	
1895	3,000	2,666	76,997	82,663	86,986	1,562		4,323
1896	3,000	2,468	109,028	114,496	102,780	13,278	11,716	
1897	3,000	2,857	72,855	78,712	51,480	26,004	27,232	
1898	3,000	2,439	20,802	26,241	30,910	20,835		4,669
1899	3,000	2,030	27,509	32,539	32,386	20,987	153	
1900	3,000	2,902	30,922	36,824	38,686	19,126		1,862
1901	3,000	3,015	28,148	34,163	35,670	17,618		1,507
1902	3,000	2,892	23,680	29,572	38,158	9,032		8,586
1903	3,000	2,791	31,895	37,685	40,745	5,973		3,060
1904	3,000	2,213	32,608	37,821	45,595			7,774
1905	3,000	2,510	49,375	54,885	54,794	91	91	
1906	3,000	2,523	45,070	50,593	50,546		47	
1907	5,000	2,257	67,170	74,427	71,900	65	2,527	
1908	5,000	2,267	57,091	64,458	60,395	129	4,063	
	$68,695	$114,051	$1,317,531	$1,538,930	$1,502,337		$83,451	$46,858

x Borrowed from State Fund, $2,763.
y   "   "   "   " , $1,610.
z Returned to   "   " , $1,049.
n Deficit due Treasurer, $1,002.
b $5,000 from L. J. Knowles' Machine Shop Fund.
c $3,000   "   "   "   "   "   "
d $4,000   "   "   "   "   "   "
In 1873, received I. Washburn Machine Shop Fund; invested same year.

WORCESTER POLYTECHNIC INSTITUTE.

STUDENTS IN ATTENDANCE

Year	Worc.	Worc. Co. (excl. City)	Worc. Co. (incl. City)	State Mass. (excl. Co.)	State Mass. (incl. Co.)	U. S. Outside Mass.	Outside State Mass.	Foreign	Total
1870–71	35	39	74	3	77	5	5	0	82
1871–72	25	38	63	12	75	14	14	0	89
1872–73	29	30	59	33	92	16	16	0	108
1873–74	40	33	73	26	99	19	19	0	118
1874–75	26	24	60	34	94	24	24	0	118
1875–76	26	27	53	26	79	14	20	6	99
1876–77	33	22	55	22	84	17	22	5	106
1877–78	35	18	53	16	69	15	18	3	87
1878–79	43	19	62	12	74	14	16	2	90
1879–80	43	15	58	16	74	18	19	1	93
1880–81	32	18	50	20	70	28	31	3	101
1881–82	34	20	54	35	89	32	33	1	122
1882–83	30	26	56	34	90	41	42	1	132
1883–84	31	30	61	34	95	41	41	0	136
1884–85	39	30	69	37	106	33	36	3	142
1885–86	45	36	81	34	115	31	38	7	153
1886–87	82	32	84	23	107	30	34	4	141
1887–88	58	35	93	27	120	33	37	4	157
1888–89	69	41	110	28	138	27	30	3	168
1889–90	79	40	119	23	142	27	29	2	171
1890–91	91	45	136	25	161	29	35	6	196
1891–92	112	57	169	33	202	34	41	7	243
1892–93	111	73	184	37	221	49	58	9	279
1893–94	92	72	164	34	198	51	59	8	257
1894–95	74	60	134	25	159	44	50	6	209
1895–96	67	48	115	34	149	46	51	5	200
1896–97	78	52	130	35	165	50	56	6	221
1897–98	79	53	132	34	166	47	50	4	216
1898–99	88	62	150	37	187	45	49	3	236
1899–1900	85	62	147	46	193	56	60	4	253
1900–01	92	62	154	53	207	59	63	4	270
1901–02	79	53	133	66	199	50	56	6	254
1902–03	83	44	127	61	188	52	60	8	248
1903–04	95	46	141	66	207	56	65	9	272
1904–05	99	45	144	93	237	78	88	10	325
1905–06	111	61	172	107	279	95	109	14	388
1906–07	110	63	173	136	309	117	129	12	438
1907–08	93	66	159	167	326	128	139	11	465
1908–09	106	71	177	154	331	142	155	13	486

A graphical representation of the above statistics up to and including the year 1904–'05, can be immediately furnished if desired.

EDMUND A. ENGLER.

Sept. 29, 1908.

WORCESTER POLYTECHNIC INSTITUTE.

Year	No. Stu. Wor. Co. incl. City	No. Stu. State excl. Co.	No. Stu. State incl. Co.	No. Stu. Total	Expend Total	W.P.I.'s contrib. to State*
1868–69	——	——	——	——	$14,504	——
1869–70	——	——	——	——	19,433	——
1870–71	74	3	77	82	17,274	$13,947
1871–72	63	12	75	89	21,017	14,504
1872–73	59	33	92	108	24,943	15,952
1873-74	73	26	99	118	26,117	17,279
1874–75	60	34	94	118	26,254	15,562
1875-76	53	26	79	99	24,901	12,385
1876–77	55	22	84	106	27,503	15,843
1877–78	53	16	69	87	23,834	15,306
1878–79	62	12	74	90	23,515	16,114
1879–80	58	16	74	93	22,793	13,730
1880–81	50	20	70	101	22,788	10,750
1881–82	54	35	89	122	22,641	9,304
1882–83	56	34	90	132	No figures	10,000(Est.)
1883–84	61	34	95	136	28,148	12,565
1884–85	69	37	106	142	29,774	14,710
1885–86	81	34	115	153	30,487	15,785
1886–87	84	23	107	141	30,656	17,769
1887–88	93	27	120	157	31,376	17,950
1888–89	110	28	138	168	31,293	19,468
1889–90	119	23	142	171	35,128	10,310
1890–91	136	25	161	196	36,857	8,618
1891–92	169	33	202	243	41,608	6,742
1892–93	184	37	221	279	48,114	7,562
1893–94	164	34	198	257	52,219	12,994
1894–95	134	25	159	209	54,960	20,693
1895–96	115	34	149	200	56,560	22,317
1896–97	130	35	165	221	59,916	19,465
1897–98	132	34	166	216	63,615	23,404
1898–99	150	37	187	236	60,214	19,135
1899–00	147	46	193	253	58,262	11,940
1900–01	154	53	207	270	61,988	12,853
1901–02	133	66	199	254	67,936	14,283
1902–03	127	61	188	248	73,892	24,700
1903–04	141	66	207	272	73,264	25,480
1904–05	144	93	237	325	77,087	21,622
1905–06	172	107	279	388	90,345	13,425
1906–07	173	136	309	437	114,275	7,950
1907–08	159	167	326	465	120,331	13,038
						575,454

* This column represents for each year the sum expended by the Institute in giving instruction to students resident in the State, in excess of the tuitions paid by them and of the sum received from the State on account of State Scholarships and of the interest at 4 per cent. on the $50,000 received from the State.

October 10, 1908.

Year	Expend.	No. Stu.	Cost per Stu.	Rec'd from State, acct. Scholarships	Cost to Institute acct. Schol.	
1868–69	$14,504	——	——	——*	——	
1869–70	19,433	——	——			
1870–71	17,274	82	$211	$2,000	$2,220	
1871–72	21,017	89	236	2,000	2,720	
1872–73	24,943	108	231	2,000	2,620	
1873–74	26,117	118	221	2,000	2,420	
1874–75	26,254	118	223	2,000	2,460	
1875–76	24,901	116	215	2,000	2,300	
1876–77	27,503	106	259	2,000	3,180	
1877–78	23,834	87	274	2,000	3,480	
1878–79	23,515	90	261	2,000	3,220	
1879–80	22,793	93	245	2,000	2,900	
1880–81	22,788	101	225	2,000	2,500	
1881–82	22,641	122	186	2,000	1,720	
1882–83	No figures	132	No figures	2,000	2,000 (Estimated)	
1883–84	28,148	136	207	2,000	2,140	
1884–85	29,774	142	210	2,000	2,200	
1885–86	30,487	153	199	2,000	1,980	
1886–87	30,656	141	217	2,000	2,340	
1887–88	31,376	157	200	2,000	2,000	
1888–89	31,293	168	186	2,000	2,720	
1889–90	35,128	171	205	2,000	2,100	
1890–91	36,857	196	188	2,000	1,760	
1891–92	41,608	243	171	2,000	1,420	
1892–93	48,114	279	172	2,000	1,440	
1893–94	52,219	257	203	2,000	2,060	
1894–95	54,960	209	263	2,000	3,260	
1895–96	56,560	200	283	2,000	3,660	
1896–97	59,916	221	271	—5,000	5,840	
1897–98	63,615	216	294	5,000	6,760	
1898–99	60,214	236	255	5,000	5,200	
1899–00	58,262	253	230	—8,000	1,200	
1900–01	61,988	270	229	8,000	1,160	
1901–02	67,936	254	267	8,000	2,680	
1902–03	73,892	248	300	8,000	4,000	
1903–04	73,264	272	290	8,000	3,600	
1904–05	77,087	325	256	8,000	2,240	95,500
1905–06	90,345	388	225	—12,000	3,000	(Gain)
1906–07	114,275	437	200	12,000	4,000	(Gain)
1907–08	120,331	465	213	12,000	3,480	(Gain)

$85,020

*This column gives for each year the sum received from the State on account of scholarships plus the interest at 4 per cent. on the $50,000 endowment received from the State.

1870–71 to 1878–79. 20 State Scholarships, tuition fee, $100.
1879–80 to 1895–96. 20 " " " " 150.
1896–97 to date. 40 " " " " 150.

October 10, 1908.

CPSIA information can be obtained
at www.ICGtesting.com
Printed in the USA
BVOW06*1219211216
471458BV00025B/55/P